Christianity in a Secularized World

Wolfhart Pannenberg

Christianity in a Secularized World

SCM PRESS LTD

Translated by John Bowden from the German
Christentum in einer säkularisierten Welt,
published 1988 by Verlag Herder, Freiburg im Breisgau

© Verlag Herder, Freiburg im Breisgau 1988

Translation © Crossroad Publishing Company 1989

334 01917 6

First published in English 1988
by SCM Press Ltd,
26–30 Tottenham Road, London N1 4BZ

Phototypeset by Input Typesetting
and printed in Great Britain by
Richard Clay Ltd, Bungay

218415

Contents

Preface   vii

1   The Dispute over Secularization and the Question
    of its Historical Causes   1

2   The Problematical Consequences of Cultural
    Secularization   21

3   The Tasks of Christian Theology in a Secular Culture   41

    Bibliography   59

Preface

Far-reaching changes in the relationship between culture and religion, in particular changes in the relationship between culture and the Christian churches, have taken place in the modern Western world. All descriptions of the situation agree here, however much they may differ in their evaluation of the process which has led to it. The way in which the world of culture has become independent from Christianity and above all from the churches has been understood as an expression of human self-assertion in the face of the claims of clerical rule, but also, conversely, as a 'loss of the centre', as an expression of apostasy from the God of the Bible. Others have seen the central idea of modern times, that of freedom, as being Christian in origin and have therefore regarded the modern 'history of freedom' as a process of the realization of Christianity itself in the world. Here, however, the form of Christianity as church has become obsolete, though the churches continue to exist as marginal phenomena. In yet another perspective the same situation is represented as the consequence of the progressive differentiation of the social system in the process of its history (N.Luhmann). Religion is said to have lost its direct responsibility for the unity of society as a whole not as a result of any historical circumstances but by virtue of the inner logic of the development of the social system; however, it still exists as a partial system in society and in so doing continues to fulfil a very important function for society as a whole. Finally, mention should also be made of those views which understand the emancipation of modern culture from religious ties as a consequence of what is alleged to be an insight into the illusory character of religion generally.

The concept of secularization has played a special descriptive role among the manifold interpretations of the relationship of the modern Western world to the mediaeval culture which had been shaped by Christianity. However, the term lacks clarity. It can be associated with a variety of evaluations. That may be one of the reasons why since around 1970 it has been moved firmly into the background of the discussion. Moreover, what has contributed to this move has been criticism of the use of the metaphor of 'secularization' as being conditioned by the standpoint of whoever uses it, so that it necessarily seemed inappropriate in any description of the relationship between modern culture and Christianity which claimed to be objective. However, this very ambivalence of the term can also commend it as a designation of so extraordinarily complex a state of affairs. This ambivalence leaves room for a variety of evaluations. Therefore the use of the term need not necessarily be bound up with a particular standpoint. On the other hand it is necessary, for the sake of clarity, to go into the dispute about the concept of secularization if one is to keep it as a summary designation of the relationship between the modern cultural world and Christianity.

To call modern culture 'secularized' can on the one hand mean that it is a world from which the holy has disappeared. On the other hand, however, it can also denote a world which continues to be linked to its Christian roots despite all its emancipation from Christianity. The criticism of secularization and its consequences is similarly ambivalent. Such criticism need not end up in the recommendation of a return to the relationship between the church and the world as it was before the modern period. However, the criticism can be rightly be rejected if it is alleged that it is based on nostalgic ideals of this kind. Any specific criticism of the consequences of secularization will take into account the fact that the break with the mediaeval model of the relationship between church and society has made possible a wealth of productive developments on which no one would seriously want to go back. These include the rights of individuals to freedom, the overcoming of authoritarian forms of rule in church and society, and cultural pluralism. Criticism of the consequences of secularization can aim at a new definition of the relationship between religion and society. But for that reason it need not just be seen as an expression of mere nostalgia or of a conservative disposition.

1 The Dispute over Secularization and the Question of its Historical Causes

The concept of secularization has its roots in the Christian distinction between the spiritual and the worldly. 'Secularization' originally had a legal meaning as a term for restoring a member of the clergy to worldly status or for the transfer of clerical goods into worldly possession. The latter process was regarded, at any rate by the Roman Catholic Church, as a strictly illegitimate act, in that it was illegal appropriation of church property. This was because of the seizure of church possessions by the worldly authorities in the Reformation period and later after the Reichsdeputationshauptschluss of 1803 ('The Final Recess of the Imperial Delegates', at which there was a major territorial reorganization in Germany associated with the necessity of ceding the right bank of the Rhine to France) even by Roman Catholic rulers. The other side could regard the same process as a sign of progress, as an abolition of unjustified privileges enjoyed by the church and a return of property withheld from Christian people to their own control or that of their political representatives.

As H.Lübbe showed in 1965, a similarly contradictory evaluation can be noted in the transfer of the concept of secularization to developments in cultural history. In his view this transferred terminology only arose after the middle of the nineteenth century. Here, too, on the one hand the slogan 'secularization' was used as a demand for the emancipation of cultural life, for example science or even moral conceptions, from the tutelage of church and theology. On the other hand there was a lament over the increasing detachment of culture generally from the church and Christianity, though up to the end of the First World War this was raised more on the Roman Catholic than on the Protestant side. Protestantism tended more to see the secularization of culture as a necessary historical process which also freed religious life from fetters which had been imposed by the Christian habits of Christian states and especially by the political establishment of a particular church as a state church.

The term 'secularization' was not used as a descriptive, value-neutral category to describe cultural developments until our century. It was used to denote the process of 'ridding the world of magic' (H.Becker, 1932) which had in fact come about in the history of modern civilization above all as a result of modern science and technology. Max Weber spoke of 'secularization' in similarly value-neutral terms, for example in his investigation of the Calvinistic roots of modern capitalism. Here he particularly had in mind the transference to the economic sphere of the virtues of the work ethic which had developed from the Calvinistic belief in predestination in connection with an ascetic life-style. These virtues proved to be the key to economic success in a completely new way.

Richard Fester spoke of a 'secularization' of the historical consciousness and historical thought as early as 1908, at a congress of historians in Berlin, in terms of 'historical thought freeing itself from the fetters of the biblical-theological world-view' (Lübbe, 56). His comments were still bound up with the solemn feelings which went with emancipation. In 1953 Karl Löwith described the modern philosophy of history in much more critical terms in his book *Weltgeschichte und Heilsgeschehen* (see in English *Meaning in History. The Theological Implications of the Philosophy of History*), as the result of a secularization of the Christian theology of history. Löwith regarded Augustine's *The City of God* as the classic document of the Christian theology of history, and discussed the French theologian Jacques-Benigne Bossuet, with his *Discours sur l'historie universelle* of 1681, as its last representative. In Löwith's view, beginning with Voltaire and culminating in Hegel's and Marx's philosophy of history, the conception of the divine providence which directs the course of history has been replaced by the idea of human progress in the historical development of the human race. Thus man or human nature becomes the subject of history in place of God. However, Löwith regarded belief in progress as an illusion. Therefore his account of the secularization of the theology of history in modern historical thought lacked the solemnity associated with emancipation. But Löwith had no intention, either, of recommending a return to the theological roots of the historical consciousness. Rather, he attacked the conception of time which is relevant both for the theology of history and for its secularized form, according to which historical time runs irreversibly towards a future goal. Löwith thought that this idea made sense only within the framework of Christian eschatology. However, the 'unfulfilled proclamation of a true eschaton with a last judgment and redemption cannot be reconciled with reason' (188). So Löwith recommended a departure from what he thought to be the overvaluation of history in Christianity and in modern times and a return to the Greek view that the nature of things and their ordering always remain the same.

I have reproduced Karl Löwith's argument in such detail because he has become the main object of the vehement attacks by Hans Blumenberg on the way in which the concept of secularization has determined the modern attitude to the period of history which preceded it. Blumenberg's book is entitled *Die Legitimität der Neuzeit* ('The Legitimacy of Modernity', 1966); this title is itself to be understood as an antithesis to the account of the origin of modern culture as the result of a secularization of Christianity. According to Blumenberg the conception of secularization implies the notion of illegitimacy. That follows from the 'expropriation model', according to which the owner is deprived of a possession which originally belonged to him. According to Blumenberg, the application of the notion of secularization to the question of the origin of modernity therefore burdens modern culture with the stigma of historical injustice. 'If in its historical existence modernity became secularity, then it would have to understand itself as an embodiment of *what it should not "as a matter of fact" be*. That would produce something like objective cultural guilt...' (73). Blumenberg therefore judges the diagnosis of the origin of modernity from a process of secularization to be a theologoumenon 'which seeks to lay the consciousness of the guilt for the onset of the ancestral heritage on the heirs of theology' (ibid.).

Blumenberg argued against Löwith that the idea of progress is in no way a feature which originally belonged to Christian theology, which was purloined from it by a 'one-sided withdrawal'. Rather, Christian eschatology and the idea of progress are quite heterogeneous conceptions. Moreover, eschatology originally had nothing to do with historical consciousness, so that historical thought was in no way an original spiritual possession of Christianity which could have been removed from Christianity by secularization. This argument of Blumenberg's is based on the assumption of an original contrast between eschatology and history, an assumption which must now be judged to be mistaken, but which at the time was

6

advanced by scholars like Bultmann and Löwith. If we follow the view that eschatology, as the future of history, is part of the understanding of reality as history and grew out of that, i.e. out of Old Testament, historical thought, then Löwith's theory that modern historical thinking originated in the Christian theology of history is much less vulnerable to Blumenberg's criticism than that of an opposition between eschatology and history, which is adopted in opposition to Löwith. In that case, all that is left of Blumenberg's critical arguments is the thesis that the idea of progress and the notion of providence are heterogeneous. But this was not in fact an objection to Löwith. In his answer to Blumenberg's criticism, Löwith pointed out that he never claimed that the idea of progress was a 'metamorphosis' of theological ideas (*Philosophische Rundschau* 15, 1968, 198). He had had nothing to do with the unhistorical conception of a 'substance which maintains itself' through a process of historical change (196). However, Löwith rightly maintained that Christian eschatology and salvation history opened up the horizon of an orientation on the future, which was then taken over by the very different idea of progress (98f.). He still saw this in effect as a 'secularization' (199). Löwith saw as virtually a 'proof' of this, albeit an indirect one, the fact that in modern times the place of the creator God had been taken by the notion of human creativity. The notion of creative human freedom would not have been possible without the idea of the biblical creator God. Humankind was first presented as the image of the divine creator, and was then to take his place (199).

Blumenberg's counter to the conception of secularization which he had rejected was that as the result of the development of the Christian conception of God in the late Middle Ages into a 'theological absolutism', man was so driven into a corner

7

that he had to turn against the Christian God by an act of human self-affirmation. The intensification of the idea of omnipotence in the Occamist teaching of the absolute power of God in conjunction with the arbitrariness of divine predestination had deprived human beings of any meaningful place in the world (132ff.), so that their only alternative had been rebellion against this God. 'Under the tremendous pressure of unreasonable theological demands the human subject began to consolidate itself. Because theology intended to represent the absolute interest of God, it allowed man's interest in himself and his concern for himself to become absolute, in other words, to take the place occupied by theological claims' (165).

However, Blumenberg's characterization of late mediaeval theology is historically untenable, as I pointed out as early as 1968 in a review of his book. Augustine's idea of absolute predestination, which foisted the decision as to the election or rejection of the individual solely on the divine will, whose eternal decision is not only hidden from human beings but precedes any human attitude, was incomparably more 'absolutist' than anything that the late Middle Ages produced. In contrast to Augustine, the mediaeval doctrine of predestination made the divine decision dependent on God's foreknowledge of human conduct, at least in respect of the negative decision to exclude someone from eternal salvation. That also applies for Duns Scotus, to whom Blumenberg wrongly attributed the idea of 'those rejected undeservedly' (140). The theological voluntarism of the late Middle Ages was far removed from the anti-human tendency which Blumenberg imputed to it. Rather, theologians like Duns Scotus and William of Occam were equally interested in the freedom of God and human freedom. At that time both were threatened by the conception in an extreme Aristotelianism, so-called Averroism, of the deter-

8

ministic closedness of a cosmic order which left room neither for the free action of God nor for human freedom. In the face of the constraints of this cosmic system, the practical influence of which is still evident in belief in destiny and the stars, late mediaeval theology defended human freedom along with that of God.

It follows from this that the relationship between modern times and the late Middle Ages must be assessed in a different way from that in Blumenberg's historical construction. Modern times did not come into being as the result of an act of human self-assertion against the absolutism of the Christian conception of God. Nothing like a rebellion against the Christian notion of God can be established in any of the great thinkers of the early modern period before Voltaire. Rather, they were mainly concerned with interpreting it in connection with a changed view of the world. The historical roots of the modern period must be sought in quite a different direction. If late mediaeval theology played its part in creating the presuppositions for the break between eras, it was not because of its conception of the absolute power of God but because of the positivism of the church's order of grace which these theologians put forward.

It is interesting how closely Blumenberg's interpretation of the origins of modernity matches the view of Karl Barth, who similarly saw the modern period – and especially the eighteenth-century image of man – as being characterized by human independence and self-assertion in the face of the Christian God. In Barth the evaluation of this process was quite the opposite to that of Blumenberg. However, both saw the situation in a similar way, though here Barth was considering a later phase of the development. Both agreed in their diagnosis of a break of epochs which was determined by human emancipation from the bond with the God of Christianity.

However, this break in epochs can now no longer be explained purely in terms of the history of ideas, as was done by Barth and especially by Blumenberg with his thesis of a rebellion of human self-assertion against the absolutism of the Christian God. This thesis is by no means the only attempt at a derivation of the origin of modernity in terms of the history of ideas. Other similar attempts at derivation, too, must be regarded as mistaken. Thus Hegel considered the modern world to be a worldly realization of the Christian freedom rediscovered by the Reformation. That is true in so far as in the sixteenth and seventeenth centuries people in the Netherlands and in England referred back to the Reformation idea of freedom to legitimate the origins of the modern idea of freedom. However, this was not just the development of the inner consistency of the Lutheran *libertas Christiana*; the occasion arose out of the political events of the time. Similarly, there is an element of truth in Friedrich Gogarten's theory of the origin of modern secular culture in the Reformation distinction between secular government and spiritual government, restricting the church to its spiritual task. This Reformation doctrine could serve to legitimate the rise of modern secular culture and especially to legitimate the emancipation of the state from religious ties. But again, it does not explain the actual process of this emancipation. Max Weber's theory that the roots of capitalism lie in the Calvinistic ethic also shares the limitations of a derivation of the modern secular world merely in terms of the history of ideas. However, Weber did not see the connection between Calvinism and capitalism as an overall explanation of the origin of capitalism but only as an indication of one factor which had become important for it.

10

But the secularization of the Calvinistic ethic so that it became subordinated to a purely worldly struggle for success simply cannot be understood properly in terms of the fact that Calvinistic virtues like the work ethic and an ascetic lifestyle could become important factors in economic success. An explanation is needed as to why this ethic no longer primarily served the spiritual end of Christian sanctification but increasingly served purely secular ends, and that cannot be derived from Calvinistic piety.

The interpretations I have mentioned above are certainly right in seeing some connection between the Reformation and the rise of the modern secular world. To that degree these views are closer to historical reality than Blumenberg's and Barth's assertion of an alleged rebellion of human self-assertion against the Christian God. But even the Reformation understanding of faith does not lead directly and consistently to the origin of the modern secular world. Rather, it was the unintended consequences of the Reformation in church history, politics and world history which created the starting point for the origin of modern secular culture. The schism ended in a period of confessionally motivated wars and civil wars which, after a prelude in Germany, the Schmalkald War of 1546/47, extended via the Huguenot wars in France and the war which began in the Netherlands in 1566 to the end of the Thirty Years' War in Germany. During the final phase of the Thirty Years' War the Puritan Revolution took place in England, beginning in 1640, which led to the execution of the English King Charles I and the dictatorship of Cromwell, and his devastating expedition to subject Ireland in 1649 and 1650.

In this period of confessional wars, in which an attempt was made more or less vainly, and only in some cases successfully, to impose unity of faith in terms of one or other of the

11

confessions, people realized that religious passion destroys social peace. Hitherto the dominant conviction had been that the unity of religion is indispensable as the foundation for the unity of society. So down to the end of the sixteenth century the ideas of tolerance and freedom of religion found no place in political thought and action. That was as true for the Protestant side as for the Catholic. Although Luther valued the freedom of the conscience so highly, he did not infer from this the demand for religious tolerance in social life any more than Calvin did. Rather, the Reformers thought that for the sake of public order and for the unity of religious confession which they called for, those who believed otherwise should leave the country and go to a territory of their confession. At any rate they were not usually burned, as in Spain, with the single exception of the execution of Servetus in Calvin's Geneva in 1553. Indeed, Luther had been so bold as to doubt whether it was in accordance with the will of the Holy Spirit to burn heretics. The papal bull *Exsurge Domine* of 1520 which was directed against him has the sorry fame that among the theses of Luther which it condemned, this sentence too is cited and condemned: '*Haereticos comburi est contra voluntatem Spiritus*' ('To burn heretics is contrary to the will of the Spirit', Denzinger, 1483). But although Luther did not want to burn any heretics, even he was a long way from the idea of political tolerance for those of other beliefs. The same was initially true for the people of the Netherlands in their struggle against Philip II of Spain. They were not fighting for tolerance but for the true faith. Only in 1572 did the circle around William of Orange formulate the idea of religious tolerance and religious freedom for the first time and proclaim it publicly, and only in the Netherlands Declaration of Independence of 1581 were these notions set down in a binding form.

The conviction that religious unity is the presupposition for social peace was widespread, and it is in this light that we should understand the attempts, extending down to the middle of the seventeenth century and beyond, to force one's own faith on others in order to produce religious unity as a foundation of social life. However, over the decades an increasing number of people came to recognize that this in fact had the opposite result, because in many cases no side was in a position to compel religious unity along the lines of its confession. The Netherlands was a pioneer instance of this insight, and under its influence the idea of religious freedom and tolerance also gained supporters in England during the Puritan revolution. This was in contrast to the Puritans themselves, who strove for a theocratic unity of faith in society along the lines of original Calvinism. Finally, with the Glorious Revolution of 1688 and the Act of Toleration in the following year, the principle of the freedom of religion was also established in England from the Netherlands.

The doubt about the view that unity of religion is indispensable and is also an effective foundation of social peace, a doubt which grew under the impact of the wars of religion in the sixteenth and seventeenth centuries, led in the seventeenth century to thinkers like Hugo Grotius and Herbert of Cherbury seeking instead the basis of social order and also of peace between states in the natural law, and in connection with that, in a natural religion common to all human beings. There arose what Wilhelm Dilthey has called the 'natural system' of the humanities: the basic concepts of law, religion, morals and politics were reformulated on the basis of the question of what is universally human, of the 'nature' of humankind. The mutually conflicting positions of belief among the Christian confessional parties were bracketted off, and in place of religion

13

based on traditional authority, that which is common to all human beings, human 'nature', became the basis of public order and social peace. That became the starting point for a secular culture in Europe. Its beginnings developed at different rates in the different countries of Europe, first in the Netherlands and then in England, and from there in the eighteenth century they also extended to the other countries and territories of Europe which still retained a state religion. But here, too, a fundamental change had already taken place in the relationship between state and religion, in that now the monarch or the state determined in his or its sovereignty what Christian confession should be the religion of the land. Thomas Hobbes formulated this dependence of state religion on the decision of the sovereign as a thesis of his political philosophy. In substance it corresponded to the regulation of the religious peace of Augsburg for Germany in 1555, which had later been summed up in the formula *cuius regio, eius religio* (in 1599 by Johannes Heinrich Stephani).

Thus even in those countries which initially continued to have a confessional unity, the religious question was subordinated to the decision of state sovereignty and therefore could be discussed on the level of political philosophy, which in turn needed the basis of natural law. So the secularization of public culture by means of the elevation of political sovereignty to being the authority which decided on the state religion also had an influence at a very early stage on those countries which still formally maintained unity of religion as the condition for the unity of society. Because the doctrine of political sovereignty, with natural law, was based on anthropology, here too in principle there had already been a shift towards basing society and public culture on the concept of the human instead of on religion.

14

That is still true of the present form of secular societies. At least in the Western democracies, human rights and thus the concept of human nature common to all individuals occupy the place which used to be given to religion. In the socialist societies the anthropology is different, but here too a particular concept of human nature forms the basis of the political unity of society.

In the later development, in contrast to the late seventeenth and eighteenth centuries, the anthropological foundation of modern society shaped by natural law has also established itself in connection with the political organization of states. The idea of human equality and equal human freedom has favoured a tendency towards the democratic transformation of the political order which because of its basis in natural law and anthropology belongs to the political religion of modern secular culture, although in fact the political reality of the party democracies has more or less marked oligarchical features. The idea of democracy has more the function of political religion than that of a description of political reality in the modern large-scale states, in which the party oligarchies have grown large because of the need to organize the masses of citizens and to motivate them to choose at elections between alternative political programmes.

Like the political structure, so too the relationship of secular culture to religion has changed further since the seventeenth century. For the pioneer thinkers of modern secular culture in the seventeenth century religion was as much part of human nature as law and morality. To begin with, the call for tolerance and freedom of religion did not relate to religion generally, but to a particular form of religious confession. In fact, Judaism apart, it related almost exclusively to the various Christian confessions. English deism even attempted to say that Christianity as such, as opposed to its confessional elaborations, was

15

identical with natural religion and was its purified form, in order to assure it that universal cultural validity which could no longer be allowed to the confessional doctrinal systems of the churches after the end of the wars of religion. However, what was in fact still a high degree of homogeneity in religious life in Europe disintegrated in the further course of the development, in the late eighteenth and nineteenth centuries. This was particularly a result of the rise of atheism, but it also came about through the extension of the principle of freedom of religion to Moslems and to adherents of religions which originated from outside the Bible. The emergence of atheism had the decisive consequence that the neutrality of public culture to differences of religious confession was now extended to religious differences of any kind on the one hand and to atheism on the other. As a consequence of this, religion was no longer seen as a constitutive element of human nature, as in the seventeenth century, but as a matter of private preference, as distinct, say, from art. A look at today's newspapers shows us what that means for the place of religion in the consciousness of our present secular culture: religion is regarded as something which is in fact there, but in principle can be dispensed with.

Morality has asserted its binding character as that which is universally human for a longer period in the consciousness of the secular world. Even in the nineteenth century it was hardly doubted that an awareness of moral norms and their binding character was part of human nature. Nietzsche's criticism of morality did not so much introduce a change in this situation as sense that it was on the way. Perhaps the effect of psychoanalysis on the dissolution of the consciousness of moral norms has been even greater. Be this as it may, today conceptions of moral norms are largely regarded as values imposed by human beings which are communicated to individuals through socializ-

16

ation and are internalized by them. So moral norms of any kind appear as an alien determination of the individual in contrast to his or her claim to self-fulfilment. There is certainly a contradiction here, because this claim similarly has a moral basis, namely in natural law. But this contradiction is hardly felt, because human rights are not regarded as moral norms like, say, the rules of sexual morality, but have the status of a quasi-religious invulnerability.

These few indications of the changes in the anthropological foundations of secular societies are meant above all to illustrate and to confirm that in fact the image of human nature in these societies has the same fundamental position for their consciousness of unity which in earlier cultures – and still in the Christian Middle Ages – was assigned to religion. As I have said, this change took place as a consequence of the destruction of social peace at the time of the confessional disputes and wars which arose out of the division in belief in the West.

In 1975 the American historian Theodore K.Rabb, from Princeton, presented a summary discussion of the many historical investigations published since the Second World War into the crises in Europe during the sixteenth and seventeenth centuries and into the historical shift and new beginning after the middle of the seventeenth century. Rabb came to the conclusion, which he formulated carefully, that the phase of confessional wars which ended in the second third of the century and especially the period of the Thirty Years' War in Germany marked a profound break in the course of European history as a whole. After this period a fundamentally new attitude was dominant in human behaviour which was governed above all by the retreat of religious intolerance. Characteristic here is John Locke's comment on the origin of his commitment to the idea of tolerance as a result of his experience of constant

17

wars and disputes: 'all those flames that have made such havoc and desolation in Europe, and have not been quenched but with the blood of so many millions' (*Two Tracts on Government*, ed. P.Abrams, Cambridge 1967, 160). Whereas political coalitions with the opponents of one's own confessional party were still extraordinary in 1631, when Richelieu made an alliance with Gustavus Adolphus of Sweden, the protest of Pope Innocent X against the 1648 Peace of Westphalia already went unheard and, as Rabb observes, that was the fate of any involvement of religion in politics from then on (81). The repeal of the Edict of Nantes in France in 1685 and the oppression of the Huguenots that went with it was a last outbreak of religious intolerance (ibid., 81f.).

The Italian Renaissance of the fifteenth century or indeed the Reformation used to be seen as the deepest break in the course of more recent European history. However, new investigations into the seventeenth century seem to show that the most important historical shift came at the end of the time of the confessional wars. At all events, the origin of the secularized order of society and the secularization of public culture in Europe goes back to the late seventeenth century rather than right back to the Renaissance. On the other hand the French Revolution did not bring about any total change and new beginning in this respect, but merely introduced a new phase in the development of the secular culture of Europe.

The results formulated by Rabb relating to the significance of the seventeenth century as a turning point in European history confirm Wilhelm Dilthey's investigations into the history of the humanities. In Dilthey's view the 'first and most powerful motive' for the reorientation of thought on universal human nature which took place in the seventeenth century is to be found in the division of the church and the destructive wars of faith. However many connections there may be with earlier ideas – with Stoic natural law, with the idea of the Renaissance and with the Reformation idea of Christian freedom – the shift towards the secular society arose out of the compulsion of need, not out of the ideas of Renaissance and Reformation, and certainly not out of a rebellion against the God of Christianity.

2 The Problematical Consequences of Cultural Secularization

In the history of Christianity there has always been a more or less marked difference between church and state, between the spiritual and the secular spheres of life. This is what makes the culture shaped by Christianity different from others, e.g. from Islamic culture. This difference between the spiritual and the secular is the expression of the eschatological awareness of the transitoriness of the order of this world, in the face of which the church with its liturgical life conveys participation in the ultimate reality of the kingdom of God, albeit in a merely symbolic, sacramental form.

In this sense the world of the mediaeval West was more strongly characterized than Byzantine culture by the relative independence of a worldly sphere of life. During the Middle Ages the awareness of the character of worldly, secular education came to be allied in a series of new waves with the revival of the legacy of antiquity. This was to a special degree the case in the Italian Renaissance, which in our present perspective no longer appears to be a quite incomparable phenomenon but rather a link in a chain of such renaissances which began as early as the Carolingian period.

The secular culture of modernity which came into being in the seventeenth century is an essentially different phenomenon. Now we no longer have the peculiarity of a secular sphere in the context of a cultural world which is wholly determined by

Christianity, but a refounding of cultural life generally on that which is universally human, leaving aside all historically conditioned religion. Accordingly, in the seventeenth century the appeal to antiquity took on a new function because it was no longer made on the basis of a culture determined by Christianity but as the model for a cultural order which was to be founded on human nature. To begin with, it was not yet very clear that as a result not only the differences between the Christian confessions but also the differences between Christianity in general and other religions were to be regarded as inessential, but it was a consequence of the new cultural approach, as was ultimately the relativization of the difference between religion in general and atheism.

The first and most important consequence of this new cultural beginning was the emancipation of the political order from its ties with Christianity. This emancipation did not immediately take the radical form of a separation of church and state. In many countries this consequence has not been reached even now, and moreover the separation of church and state can have differing significance. It can be aimed at restricting religion to the private sphere, as was the case at the beginning of the French Revolution and in Russia after the October Revolution. But it can also have the significance of preventing political authorities from intervening in the religious decisions of citizens and in the churches' competition with one another, as has been the case in the USA. Only recently have the rulings of the Supreme Court in the USA developed a tendency to interpret the American constitution in such a way that religion is treated as a private matter, and the controversy over this is still in full swing. The emancipation of the political order from its ties to Christianity can thus emerge in many forms. But even in countries in which a Christian confession has been established as the state religion, it has been subordinated to reasons of state, as was already the case in the seventeenth century in Richelieu's France. In later phases the preservation of the form of the state church can even have the function of providing better control of church life by the authorities, who have obligations towards religious agnosticism or atheism, as in Sweden or the German Democratic Republic. In between lie countries which accord a certain degree of privilege and public recognition to those churches which represent a majority of the population. Even here, however, in the advanced stages of the development of modern secular culture Christianity no longer has any determining influence on the way in which the political order understands itself as such, however much those who are part of it may feel personal ties to one of the Christian churches.

In modern history the emancipation of state order from ties to Christianity has at least at times been associated with the tendency of the state in its own interest to claim supreme and unlimited authority over the life of its citizens. That was the case at the time of the absolute monarchy, and also later in the forms of a more democratic nationalism. However, this tendency worked against the development of a system of individual rights to freedom by the Netherlands and England.

A further and very decisive consequence of the emancipation of the political order from religious ties is the way in which public educational institutions and the content of education have become independent of religion. However, these consequences emerge only in the further course of the history of secular culture. In some countries even now they have not resulted in a total exclusion of religious instruction from public schools or in the abolition of theological faculties at public universities. But even where these conclusions have not been drawn, religion appears only as a special theme alongside other specialities and is no longer basic to public education generally. When we add the fact that religious instruction is more concerned to be an introduction to religion for members of a particular church than information about the Christian doctrine of faith, its biblical roots and the dominant influence of Christianity on the development of European culture, it is hardly surprising that particularly in our century there has been a rapid decline in knowledge of Christianity and its basic relevance for the history of European culture, going back over centuries.

A further consequence of the emancipation of public life from religious ties, which is significant for the development of modern culture, is the autonomous dynamic which has been set in motion by economic developments and its dominant influence on the cultural consciousness. After the ending of church restrictions like the canonical prohibition on levying interest which the Calvinists among the Reformed churches had already ceased to observe, and the lapse of the demand that economic activity should be subordinated to other goals in the service of society and should not follow the mere pursuit of gain, the development of the economy was initially hindered in the mercantile period by state regulations; however, under the banner of rising liberalism it was able increasingly to develop its autonomy. As a result of the association of industrial manufacture with the further development of technology and finally also of research, the autonomous dynamic of economic development intensified and increasingly influenced the social system as a whole. Although this autonomy, which was the substance of the description of capitalism in Marx, has again been channelled more strongly by political conditions, including social aims, since the end of the nineteenth century, the dominant significance of economics in modern secular society has led to a wide-ranging commercialization of cultural activity and not least to a consumer approach to culture. The products of culture are marketed, and cultural consumption is manipulated through advertising. This development has steadily changed the relationship to the content of cultural tradition, positively from the perspective of a much wider scope for individual preferences, and negatively in the sense of a loss of the binding nature of the content of cultural tradition, because the commercial attitude is to treat it as consumer goods which are interchangeable more or less at will.

Even religion is not immune from the dangers of commercialization. That was already evident from the trade in indulgences in the early sixteenth century which became the occasion for Luther's Ninety-Five Theses. The most recent scandal over television evangelism in the USA is another example. Nevertheless, on the whole religion is far less affected by the commercialization of cultural life than art and literature. That means that it suffers all the more from the changed attitude to our cultural heritage as a result of this commercialization. For nowhere are the obligations and claims of tradition so strong and so inalienable as in the case of religion. One cannot take the matter of religion, and especially Christianity, seriously without exposing oneself to its obligations and claims. Therefore a consumer attitude to cultural tradition is particularly incompatible with religious life.

According to Max Weber the repression of traditional and value-rational attitudes by the extension of purposive rational behaviour is primarily resposible for the secularization of cultural forms of life. Though this purposive rationality may also have one of its roots in Calvinist ethics, its cultural rise to becoming the dominant form of behaviour in the modern world has nevertheless been most closely bound up with the development of capitalist economics and technology. Therefore Weber also expected that the further development of modern industrial society would increasingly force religion to the periphery of social life. He regarded this process of 'the abolition of magic' as an inevitable historical destiny.

Since then this view has been a dominant influence in the discussion of the secularization of modern society. It was also shared by the American sociologist Peter Berger when he wrote his book *A Rumor of Angels* in 1969. In contrast to Weber, as a committed Christian Berger lamented the inevitability of the progress of secularization in European and American culture. But he regarded the trend as irreversible, because the advance of secularization was a cultural concomitant of modern industrial society (20). For the adherents of religion this meant that they had to accept the status of cognitive minorities who had consciously to oppose massive pressure to assimilate to the social environment in order to maintain their commitment.

Some years later, however, in 1973, Berger and others published an investigation which led them to other conclusions. The title of the book, *The Homeless Mind*, already indicates this. Berger's thesis is that the increasing 'modernization' of society, which is decisively characterized by industrialization and bureaucratization, inevitably produces effects which hinder its further progress and which become all the stronger, the further the process of modernization proceeds. The process of the development of secular culture in the sense of the constant advance of 'modernization' thus comes up against inner limits. That means that one cannot count on an unlimited increase in secularization, as Max Weber assumed.

Berger sees the inner limits of secularization being set in particular by the individual's need for meaning: individuals

28

need to interpret the reality in which they live in a meaningful way, in order to be able to feel that their own life is meaningful (15). But modern secular culture does not satisfy this need for meaning. Max Weber certainly saw the problem, but treated it more as a marginal phenomenon. Berger attached far more importance to it.

According to his account, individuals play their particular roles in the world of work, but in doing so remain largely anonymous. Moreover it is often impossible for individuals to see interconnections in the world of work and also in society as a whole. So they experience the social system, too, as an anonymous power, despite the changing faces of those who hold office in it. The bureaucratic control of social life reinforces this situation in both directions: the bureaucracy regards the individual as an instance of abstract categories without taking note of his or her individuality, and the individual sees bureaucracy as the manifestation of an anonymous power complex. Its decisions are largely felt to be arbitrary, even if this view is not held about individual officials in the bureaucracy but more about the system of rules and regulations by which they have to order their decisions. The principle of equal treatment regardless of individual circumstances leads, as Berger puts it, to a climate of 'moralized anonymity' (52). The individual citizen feels impotent in the face of this (60), although the bureaucracy is supposed to be doing its best.

In addition to this there is the pluralization of the world in which we live through the division between public and private spheres, and also the plurality of institutions within the public sphere. Each of them forms a world in itself, so that individuals have to move to and fro between different worlds. The integration of this plurality of aspects of the world, which used to be achieved by religion, no longer takes place in the public world of secular culture but has to be achieved by the individual. The basis of this is meant to be the private sphere of life, the world of the family. But in many cases this cannot stand up to the burdens imposed by modern life. The growth of urban living has contributed to an increase of pluralization in the private sphere also, making the task of integration increasingly difficult.

According to Berger, this situation leads more and more often to experiences of frustration (69, 73), to permanent crises of identity for the individual (78), and finally to a feeling of 'homelessness' in the social world (82). Nor can religion offer a way out of this situation, because it is itself threatened by pluralization (79), namely by the plurality of religious or ideological systems of meaning which the individual encounters and the truth-claims of which reciprocally relativize themselves for him. For this reason alone the religious tradition has largely lost its plausibility (184f.), but the problems of individual living which in the past were solved by religion, especially the experiences of suffering and evil in the world, remain and are constantly renewed (185). Indeed they are even intensified by the anonymity of modern secular society and culture, and by their pressures.

The effects of secular culture on the individual consciousness in the experience of homelessness in this world leads to reactions against the system of public culture and society which extend from the development of counter-cultures in industrial societies, especially among the young, to the demand for liberation from the institutional pressures of society and the alienation which goes with this, an alienation which is thought to be especially associated with the capitalist economic system (195). The expectation that the freedoms granted in the private sphere will compensate for the frustrations which individuals

30

experience in the public world of secular culture and especially in the world of work is realistic only up to a point, because the dissatisfaction is also with the division between public and private life (229). Individual reactions extend from a flight into an irrational counter-world, e.g. the so-called youth sects, to violence against a social system which is felt to be repressive.

Significantly, Berger observes that the resistance in Third World countries to a 'modernization' of the Western type has the same motivation as the reactions of the sub-cultures and youth cultures against the system of secular culture in the industrial countries themselves. The increase in standard of living, individual freedom and life-expectation which at least for some is associated with modernization is certainly also attractive in Third World countries. But on the other hand, here too the dissolution of traditional orders of life and the loss of meaning associated with it are felt to be threats to the individual.

In the years since the appearance of his book, new events and developments have taken place which can be regarded as confirmation of Berger's diagnoses: the resistance to the secular culture of the West in Third World countries has found its most visible and effective expression in the revival of a fundamentalist and militant Islam. In the industrial countries themselves the environmental crisis has sharpened the awareness of the limits of industrial and technological progress and indeed has even begun to bring about such awareness in broad areas of the population. But Berger's scepticism about the possible effectiveness of reactions to the process of moderniz-ation, above all in the advanced industrial countries, also seems to be confirmed: these societies cannot get out of the process of modernization, industrialization and technological develop-ment without causing unheard-of suffering and impoverishment and possibly the death of millions (216). Therefore in Berger's view it is probable that the reactions against modernization will remain parasitical phenomena of a flight into irrational counter-worlds, with those who hold such views themselves being dependent on the living conditions of industrial society (222f.) and claiming its attractive features for themselves.

However, that does not mean that the existence of secular society and its culture is stable. Its great defect, to which Berger has constantly referred, is the loss of any meaningful focus of commitment in the spheres of public culture and private life. In former cultures a meaningful focus of commitment was provided by religion. The loss of such a focus as a result of the detachment of public culture from ties to a particular form of religion initially brought individuals great freedom and thus also introduced a phase of cultural flowering. However, this cultural flowering in the eighteenth and nineteenth centuries still lived on the aftermath of the cultural tradition, the basic elements of which were all present, even though the age itself had diverged from its norms. In advanced secular society, the presence of these basic elements has faded in human consciousness. That applies not only to Christianity but also to the legacy of antiquity and its influence on European culture. True, information about these elements is still available, but as a culture to be consumed, along with a variety of other items on offer. Whether to make use of them is left to individual preference, especially as the educational system no longer presents them as being binding. The arbitrariness of the consumption of culture destroys any sense of the binding nature of the cultural tradition and especially the religious tradition. But people need to be orientated on that which gives binding meaning. Erich Fromm has spoken of the need for a referential

32

framework to provide orientation on the world, and along with this of the need for respect towards the sources and vehicles of such an orientation (*The Revolution of Hope*, 1968, 62). Without such an orientation that is binding on the individual everything can become a matter of indifference. And in that case hopelessness and feelings of alienation spread under cover of succumbing to the pressures of the consumer society.

I now want to go on to pay particular attention to three aspects of the long-term effects of the secularization of culture.

First of these is the loss of legitimation in the institutional ordering of society. In earlier periods of cultural history the most important function of religion for the cultural ordering of society was that religion preserved and communicated the consciousness of the divine origin of the world and thus also of society and its order. The divine reality worshipped in religion is exalted above human manipulation. Precisely for that reason, and because it is the origin of the human world, it can also be the criterion for the ordering of social life, on which that life has to orientate itself and by which it is also legitimated. That is true of all social institutions, but especially of particular forms of political rule and the exercising of them. Without such legitimation, political rule would be merely the exercising of power, and citizens would then inevitably feel that they were delivered over to the whim of those who had power. With the collapse of the religious foundation of the cultural order the danger arises that the legitimation of political rule is lost and that the *de facto* conditions of rule then seem to be the oppression of individuals by those who happen to hold power. The political philosophy of the seventeenth and eighteenth centuries sought to obviate such views by social contract theories, which derive the fact of political rule from human nature, in so far as political rule guarantees a state of civic legal peace which individuals must affirm as also being of advantage to themselves. Particular forms of political rule are not themselves, of course, to be derived from that. Now in the notion of representative democracy a model of political order was developed, based on the natural-law concept of equal freedom for individuals, and associated with the idea of their common sovereignty. However, we reach the critical point of the concept of representative democracy with the question whether and under what conditions those who perform political functions in fact represent the common will of the electorate in the exercise of these functions. Under the conditions of modern secular culture it is increasingly difficult to guarantee the necessary degree of identification between the electorate and their elected representatives. The mere fact of general elections at intervals of several years is not enough for that. The actual influence of the electorate on political events is indeed minimal. That is even true for most members of political parties. So even in democratic societies the political system can easily be felt to be repressive, especially since in the world of secular culture the claims of public institutions on individuals can easily appear as constraints which are laid on them by society.

That need not be the case as long as it is possible for individuals to identify with the institutional ordering of society by means of their consciousness of law. In the case of the political order, such an identification could come about by means of their link with the constitution, provided that individual citizens can identify with the constitution of their country. However, state constitutions are themselves products of the human will. Moreover, the details of them are constantly changed. Furthermore in secular cultures even the notion of law has lost its religious foundations. The replacement of this by the idea of natural law has the defect that natural law does

34

not directly make its mark on the specific form of the legal order. The specific legal order is continually subject to changes made by those who hold political power. That is true to a limited degree even of constitutional law. The legal order can therefore be regarded only conditionally as being independent over against the political situation. To the same degree, however, law loses the power to legitimate political rule. The consequence is the situation which has been described in the past few decades as the collapse of legitimacy and the legitimacy crisis of the secular state. In the last resort this legitimacy crisis is rooted in the loss of the religious foundation of the authority of the law and constantly flares up in experiences of state rule justifying itself by manipulating public awareness.

The collapse of the universal validity of traditional morality and consciousness of law is the second aspect of the long-term effects of secularization which need to be discussed more closely. In the earlier period of the secular society, in the seventeenth century, it was thought possible to ground the awareness of moral norms, independently of the religious tradition of Christianity, on the nature of man as a rational being, i.e. on natural law. In the seventeenth century this also included a knowledge of God which was supposedly bound up with human nature. Even Rousseau regarded religious faith in some form as an indispensable condition for moral norms with a binding character. Kant then taught an autonomy of moral awareness, moral norms which were binding even without religion, although he regarded belief in God as a necessary consequence of the moral consciousness and even recognized the religious sanctioning of morality in the reality of history as a condition for the realization of moral conditions. Moreover Kant's moral philosophy can be seen as a modified doctrine of natural law, and the categorical imperative in particular as a

35

modified form of the golden rule. Without the background of this tradition the formalism of Kant's foundation for morality is open to considerable objections, because while tying action to the possibility of universalizing rules for action is in accord with the modern notion of rational human freedom, it is not in accord with the individual nature of this freedom, i.e. with the claim to having the right to one's own special nature and thus to individual self-fulfilment. For each individual, with his or her own specific character, to claim a right to freedom which was originally grounded in natural law, and along with that to claim the right to unlimited self-fulfilment of his or her own particular nature, makes all moral and legal rules of conduct seem a burdensome pressure. One may adapt to it externally, but without inner conviction. In that case legal and moral norms function only like traffic regulations. In Kant's language, that means that while legal conduct may come about even without religion, morality does not derive directly from the autonomy of individual freedom. The conformity of so-called 'externally-directed behaviour' corresponds completely to the collapse of the consciousness of moral norms.

An end to attaching any binding character to moral norms has certainly been favoured by psychoanalytical interpretation which sees them as an expression of the demands of society on individuals, which are internalized by them. However, this interpretation and the associated notion that these internalized norms have the function of repressing the pleasure-principle as the root of the drive towards individual self-fulfilment, meet up with the feeling of homelessness and alienation which individuals in a secular culture experience generally in their relationship to the institutional order. In that case morality appears as an expression of social repression.

The opposition of individual freedom to all institutional

rules and claims on the individual can also be directed against the institution of the family: in the case of children against the authority of parents and in the case of parents against the ties and limitations to individual freedom which are bound up with marriage and family. However, where the context of marriage and family is destroyed, the individual is threatened with solitude, especially at a later stage of life.

This brings us to a third aspect of the long-term consequences of the secularization of culture which needs to be mentioned. The individual in his or her struggle towards orientation and identity is hardest hit by the loss of a meaningful focus of commitment, a loss which results from the secularization of culture. This loss can only be compensated for to a limited extent by individual appropriation of the content of the cultural tradition. In many cases the loss of a meaningful focus of commitment does not just lead to the experience of homelessness and alienation in a culture but also to neurotic deviations. That has been rightly stressed by Victor Frankl. Moreover, the high suicide rate may be connected with the fact that many people doubt whether their life has any meaning, not only because of particular features in their individual life history but also because of the lack of any meaningful focus of commitment in the social world of our secular culture.

In the early phases of the development of secular culture many people experienced the detachment of modern society from religious ties and the ever-advancing abolition of the limits to individual conduct which have their origin in such ties as an extension of the opportunities for individual freedom. In this sense they welcomed it as emancipation from the limits to human development imposed from outside. This insight doubtless has much to be said for it, even in the sphere of religion. The pluralism of cultural life, the freedom of science and art, and not least the increasing pluralism in religious life, could work as an enrichment. But they also have shadow sides, the origin of which seems to lie in the loss of a meaningful focus of commitment in cultural and social life. These consequences have remained concealed for a long time, but emerge in the progressive phases of the development of secular culture.

Are there possibilities of countering such unwanted consequences of secularization? No one can want a simple return to the relationship between religion, state and culture as it was before the modern period, quite apart from the fact that such a return could not be achieved. Most of us do not want to give up the positive values of tolerance, individual self-development and the plurality of cultural forms associated with this. The question is whether there can be a renewal of the context of our culture with its religious origins which preserves the values of the modern cultural development while at the same time taking more notice of the Christian shaping of our cultural tradition in present-day cultural and political life and restoring its validity as an index of the identity of our culture.

That is a question which must be raised by anyone who is concerned for the ongoing existence of this secular culture. The increasingly evident long-term effects of the loss of a meaningful focus of commitment have led to a state of fragile equilibrium in the system of secular society. The loss of legitimation for social institutions must not lead at the same time to the collapse of the social system. As long as the social system secures an acceptable level of material prosperity for the majority of individuals, its existence need not be endangered from within, despite the spread of neuroses and feelings of homelessness and loss of meaning. But such a system is less capable of bearing burdens in times of crisis. Therefore responsible politicians should want the inner stability of the cultural and social system to be strengthened. The most obvious way, and the one which holds forth most hope of success, would be to strengthen the identity of our culture, which is grounded in its religious roots.

3 The Tasks of Christian Theology in a Secular Culture

Corrections to the secularism of modern Western culture and society cannot and should not start from the churches. Any attempt in this direction would immediately be interpreted as producing the danger of a desire for clerical control. Even if it were only to be passed over as insignificant, it would end up confirming prejudices which played a part in the early phases of the formation of secular culture. If there are to be corrections to the system of secular society and culture, then they must be weighed up and (if the occasion arises) carried through by those involved in politics, and from a political perspective.

The Roman Catholic Church has long opposed cultural secularization, and in some questions, as for example today that of the legalization of abortion, opposition is in fact necessary. But the attempts to stem the development of secular culture have not been much use. Nor have the churches any occasion to be alarmed, in the interest of their own future, by the progress of secularization. Secular culture itself produces a deep need for meaning in life and therefore also for religion. The anxiety that the progress of secularization will turn religion into a peripheral phenomenon which increasingly fades away can now be said to be unfounded and obsolete. However, it is true of public awareness in secular culture that religion is not taken seriously as a determinative human theme. Neither in the media nor in the educational system nor in politics is it given

43

its due place. Therefore the status of religion is not particularly high in many people's awareness and practices. But that does not mean that the religious theme is disappearing from human life. It is being repressed from consciousness, but it is present as the need to give meaning to life and as a sense of alienation in the secular world – indeed this need and alienation are very intensely present, although it is often not recognized that what is missing here is in fact religion.

It is difficult in secular culture to make the transition from the implicit presence of the religious theme to an explicit religious attitude because the contents of faith, particularly those of the Christian tradition, have been denied any objective binding force in the secular consciousness. Therefore faith appears as irrational commitment to a content which is regarded as 'true' only in a private perspective. Religious need can therefore easily assume the form of irrational commitment if it is recognized and affirmed as such by people. However, such a commitment can be just as binding to other contents as to that of Christianity. The fact that it is made to Christian belief is then primarily conditioned by a person's life history, say a Christian religious socialization received in childhood but later pushed into the background. At all events, in the light of secular awareness the step towards an explicit commitment in faith looks like a leap into the irrational.

So how should the churches conduct themselves in the world of a secular culture in order to make it easier for people to move from the implicit presence of the religious theme in their lives to an explicit Christian commitment of faith? What can theology contribute to this?

The possible strategies on the part of the churches and theology towards secular culture extend from the various forms of assimilation to a move in precisely the opposite direction.

Both the extreme alternatives here seem to me to be false. The resolute course away from assimilation which has been attempted in Catholic integralism or traditionalism, or on the Protestant side in the theology of Karl Barth and his school, can make an impression on people and at least in passing even on the public awareness of secular culture. Particularly in times of cultural crisis like the years after the First World War and in another way also after the Second, people have been susceptible to authoritarian claims and demands because they promise firm ground in a world which at least for the moment does not provide any support. The authoritative affirmation of religious truth is imposing by virtue of the impression of self-assurance that it gives, and its message of judgment on a world which is in any case felt to be collapsing or broken is a plausible one. But the authoritarian position is very much less impressive in the face of a secular world which is still functioning more or less. For it puts the believer into an alien atmosphere which is not conveyed by the everyday world and its criteria of reality except perhaps through the demand for radical change. Moreover left-wing Barthianism, for example, derives its impressiveness from the demand for radical change, which makes the theology of diastasis and its political programme seem topical. However, its activism provides only an apparent link with reality as it is experienced, because it goes directly against the reality that is to hand, and therefore if the radical change it seeks actually came about, the results would be quite different from what its supporters expect.

The opposite strategy is that of assimilation to the secular understanding of reality. This is thought to be a possible way of bringing people who live in the modern secularized world to faith as a possibility of understanding themselves in this world without actually having the presumption to take a leap

45

from it into a quite different world, the world of faith – a leap which can never in fact completely leave this world, so that the leap rather goes through the existence of believers themselves. The strategy of assimilation to the secular understanding of reality seeks to avoid this situation, which Hegel already described under the title of the 'unhappy consciousness'. But in so doing it risks giving up the decisive content of the tradition of faith, so that in some cases the content of faith becomes so empty that the question arises why one should still turn to religion at all. If one hears from the pulpit only what one can read in newspapers or get from psychology courses at the local college, why still go to church? Something is expected there which the secular world does not offer, namely religion. Often, however, it happens that those who have to represent the cause of religion by virtue of their office have been so unsettled by the spirit of secular culture that they think that they can serve the faith by concealing its content completely under the cloak of secularity, thus making it almost invisible. So the strategy of assimilation is largely the expression of the problems of those who hold office in the church.

This problem also has its parallels on the level of theology. Theology contributes to the training of those who hold office in the church by producing this uncertainty in them. However, the fault is not always that of theology itself; often it also lies in an inadequate acceptance and understanding of its questions and results in the course of theological study. This study is not just meant to pass on an indoctrination which is then to be handed down in sermons and teaching. Rather, study is meant to make possible the forming of independent judgments, so that the future minister of the church can put forward the truth of the Christian faith independently. To that end students must be taught to argue with the content of the tradition. Here it is

46

necessary not only to discuss the problems in the sphere of biblical criticism which have been thrown up by modern criticism of the tradition, i.e. historical-critical exegesis and the criticism of dogma; theology must also take over the truth-content of such criticism of the tradition. It is much to the credit of modern theology that the critical examination of the tradition of faith has been carried out and discussed not only from outside, but above all within theology, so that it can rightly be objected to all criticism expressed from outside that where its concerns are in fact justified, they have been perceived with far greater sophistication within the theological discussion in the form of a self-criticism of the tradition of faith. Such self-criticism does not amount to a surrender of the content of the tradition. Nevertheless, in some cases it may be that this in fact happens. In view of the complex nature of the topics under discussion this is often difficult for the student to see, and can lead to uncertainty. However, the uncertainty is usually not immediately about a personal commitment of faith so much as about the content of the tradition of faith. This explains why it is the central content of faith – the resurrection of Jesus, the trinitarian understanding of God and the doctrine of the incarnation – which is so often presented only in a restrained way in preaching.

I shall now go on to discuss some examples of such excessive assimilation of theology to the secularism of modern culture.

1. One such example, which is at the same time interesting because it is concerned with the theological thematization of secular culture, is the formula of the 'death of God' in this modern secular culture. This formula was introduced poetically by Jean Paul and philsoophically by Hegel in 1803 as a cipher for modern secular culture. It describes the world in which the autonomous self which needs no transcendent foundation

merely stands over against things as its objects, a world in which all reality is finite and the finite is absolute, and so at the same time everything is nothing, because by definition the finite ends and that is its true being. That is the world in which God is dead. In this world of nothingness God is seen to be dead because only finite realities, things and subjects are acknowledged to have reality. That is only possible if human beings, finite selves, make themselves infinite, and thus take the place of God. So for secular culture (in the 'new time', as Hegel puts it), God is dead because human beings have taken the place of God by making the human self infinite and contrasting everything else with it as finite. That is a very profound diagnosis of the metaphysical nature of modern culture. But it is only illuminating as a statement about God if the present state of the cultural world is bound up with the being of God in such a way that it can be expressed as an event which affects God himself. This conception of the 'speculative Good Friday, which otherwise was historical' comes at least very close to a pantheistic identification of the world with the divine life. The fascination which this notion has exercised on theology is probably to be explained from the fact that it makes a description of the character of secular culture in theological language possible. In that very way, it may seem, the secularism of the secular consciousness is transcended. But the price paid for this is too high. In the case of the philosophy of the early Hegel it consists in giving up the transcendence of God over against the world. Here Hegel's view was that while God is dead in secular culture, he is experienced in the impending cultural renewal of his resurrection, namely through what Hegel in his doctrine of the infinite as the absolute idea in contrast to the finitude of human subjectivity envisaged as the justification of the religious consciousness. This expectation was no longer shared in the subsequent period. Since Feuerbach had described all the divine properties as anthropomorphic transference and thus also the idea of the divine subject itself as a mere human projection, the 'new man' in Nietzsche's *Joyful Science* (1882) asserted that God is in fact dead and remains dead, having been killed by man (Aphorism 125). That, too, is a statement about the nature of secular culture or about the fact that 'belief in the Christian God has become incredible', as Nietzsche observed by way of explanation in a later aphorism (343). Christian theology cannot allow such a statement to stand as a statement about God, but only as a statement about the nature of secular culture. If need be it can speak of an 'absence' of God from the world of this culture, but only in the sense that God is absent *for the person* who has turned away from him. The Bible also knows such an absence of God from human beings regardless of the ceaselessly efficacious presence of the creator in every breath of his creatures. If God appears to human beings to be absent, although they depend on his sustaining their life at every moment of their existence, that means that they have turned away from the divine source of their life and are close to death. For God to hide himself and leave men and women to do as they fancy is an expression of his anger (Ps.89.47). Therefore the pious man prays, 'Hide not thy face from me, that I be not like those who go down to the pit' (Ps.143.7). The experience of the absence of God announces the imminence of his judgment, for according to Paul the divine judgment consists in the fact that God leaves the sinner and the world to themselves, that he 'hands them over' to the consequences of their actions.

That is how Christian theology must speak of the phenomenon that Hegel and Nietzsche have described as the death of God in modern secular culture. However, theology should not

49

itself take over the formula of the death of God and seek some metaphysical profundity in it, as happened among the American 'Death of God' theologians in the 1960s. That is excessive assimilation to the secularism of the modern world. It is in no way justified by the fact that the Christian message is the word of the cross. The death of Jesus on the cross is not the death of God, nor even the death of the Son in contrast to Father and Spirit. The dogmatically correct way of expressing the theological tradition is rather that the Son of God died on the cross in accordance with the human nature that he assumed. It has been rightly stressed in the most recent theological discussion that the God of Christian faith may not be thought of as untouched by the death of Jesus in his eternal Godhead, any less than the incarnation is to be imagined as an event external to the Godhead of the Son. The Godhead of God himself is at risk in the death of Jesus, the Godhead of the Son, but therefore also that of the Father, who would not be Father without the Son. However, that does not mean that God himself died on the cross, but that he has affirmed his Godhead against the death on the cross – the Godhead of the Son which is also that of the Father and the Spirit – by the resurrection of Jesus. If one wants to compare the aversion of secular culture from the Christian God with the crucifixion of Jesus, as happened in Hegel, in theological terms it has to be said that in the Easter event God already victoriously affirmed his deity, and that he will finally affirm it on the Last Day in judgment upon the world.

2. A second example of an excessive assimilation of Christian theology to the spirit of secular culture is the theology of demythologizing. Alternatively one could also mention the contemporary fashion of resorting again to mythical imagery, a recourse which either has purely aesthetic significance, is

an expression of romantic nostalgia, or in terms of Jungian psychology functions as compensation for the cold intellectual culture of the secular world. At all events, the recourse to myth seems to have the significance of an escape from secularity experienced as alienation into the irrational. In contrast to this, the programme of demythologizing is an assimilation of the Christian proclamation to the Spirit of modernity. In Bultmann its presupposition was that faith has nothing to do with a world-view, but only with existential human self-understanding. Bultmann used the term 'mythological' to denote the expression of faith in terms of a world-view. One may argue over whether the term 'myth' was a happy choice here and whether its use by Bultmann corresponds with its use elsewhere in the study of religion. But that is incidental here. More important is the judgment that all notions connected with a world-view are irrelevant to theology. That leads to the abandonment of any conception of a creation of the world and of eschatology as a real future involving the end of the world and its transformation. It also leads to a renunciation of the realism of Christian Easter faith and the Christian resurrection hope. The elimination of all features of a world-view from Christian conceptions of faith was matched positively by the limitation of faith to the subjectivity of existential self-understanding. That is where the assimilation to the spirit of secular culture lies, for the subjectivity of the private individual is precisely the place which secular culture gives to religion while disputing all its claims that its statements have objective truth. Pietism, or its late form, revivalist piety, has retreated into this enclave of subjectivity as the place of religion, and Bultmann's theology, like that of his teacher Wilhelm Herrmann, had its spiritual origin in this radical subjectivism which made the act of the decision of faith the basis for all certainty of truth about the content of faith, but precisely for that reason could regard any content as secondary. This is matched in Catholic thought by the danger of a fideistic supranaturalism. Over against this Christian theology must insist that the world of universal human experience is the creation of God. If God could not truly be understood as the creator of this world, then the truth of belief in the one God would be threatened. But if God is the creator of the world, then we may expect that no phenomenon of the finite reality of this world, including human beings, is appropriately understood so long as it is seen apart from its relationship to God. That is the principal counter-position to the secular consciousness which theology has to develop and defend in critical dialogue with the natural sciences and the humanities. The secular investigation of the reality of the world and human nature apart from God can be seen only as an *approximation* to the true reality of nature and humankind, and cannot be regarded as adequate *knowledge* of this reality, if the biblical idea of God is to be maintained. That means that theology, in dialogue with the sciences, has the task of demonstrating in specific terms the dimension which has thus been omitted from the phenomenon which the sciences are investigating, through which these phenomena are associated with God as the creator of the world. I have attempted to do that for the humanities, and I am confident that the same thing is possible in a dialogue with the natural sciences. Thus contrary to Bultmann's theological programme, theology must lead to discussion of the modern understanding of the world with the secularism of modern culture. That does not mean that it would have to hold on to the ancient conceptions of the world which have found expression in the biblical writings. Human beings' understanding of the world and themselves is relative to historical conditions; it is therefore changeable and also capable of progress in knowledge. Christian faith is not established by following Gen.1.6f. in imagining the firmament as a fixed heavenly vault by which the water of a heavenly ocean is prevented from falling on the earth. Nor need we suppose in a heavy rainfall that someone has forgotten to close the windows in this heavenly vault. But it is not enough to laugh at such notions if we are incapable of making specific statements about the relationship between the reality of nature and the reality of God in terms of modern knowledge. The mistake of the theology of demythologizing is not that it pointed out the historical relativity of the aspects of a world-view to be found in biblical statements, but that it disputes that faith in God has any relevance for understanding the world. That is where it begins to be excessive assimilation to the secularism of modern culture and science.

I should mention two further examples of such excessive assimilation. They are not matters of principle to the same extent but are more clearly connected with the fashions and tendencies of the age.

3. The first of these examples is feminism in theology. Not everything which goes with this phenomenon can be dismissed as false assimilation to the spirit of the time. Rather, it is true that our cultural tradition has been to a large degree moulded by a patriarchal family order which is now seen to be collapsing. It is also true that despite the patriarchal constitution of the family to be found in it, the Old Testament, i.e. biblical Judaism, already gave a higher position to the woman in family life than was the case in other cultures of antiquity, e.g. among the Greeks. Moreover, with his criticism of the one-sided right of the husband to divorce and the openness of his dealings with women generally, Jesus went still further towards revising social discrimination against women. These are facts which can be seen more clearly today than in former centuries. In some

respects the church down its history has fallen behind the beginnings of equality of the sexes that we find with Jesus and earliest Christianity. To this, of course, I also add the exclusion of women from the priestly ministry of the church. Like Karl Rahner, I see no compelling dogmatic reason which would prohibit the ordination of women. Thus theological feminism has indisputable elements of truth. But I feel that it is unacceptable that a revision should be called for in addressing God as Father on the grounds of our changed views about the position of woman in society. The biblical notion of God as Father does not assign him any sexually determined role, but has its point of comparison in the father's function of providing care and the associated authority which fell to the father as head of the family group. Jesus's use of the term 'Father' in addressing God in prayer does not indicate an interchangeable conception of God. It is Jesus' name for God and thus is part of the historical identity of Christianity. It is no more interchangeable than the historical person of the Jew Jesus himself. The idea that the image of God in the tradition has been shaped by human social conditions and therefore that changes in social conditions – as here the changed position of women – must necessarily result in changes in the image of God seems naively to presuppose that changes in religious conceptions are a function of social changes. That is to overlook the autonomy in the development of the great deities in the history of religion and is more or less involuntary confirmation of the basic conception of the modern atheistic criticism of religion that human ideas of God and gods are merely *reflections* of human relationships, and that changes to them are reflections of changes on a human level. That is the element of assimilation to the spirit of secularism.

A last example of this is liberation theology. Here, too, to

54

begin with it must be said that there are indeed social conditions the injustice of which cries out to heaven and in which there is a need for remedial help and change. That may also be called 'liberation', although Christian theology must always remain mindful of the fact that the deepest servitude of human beings is servitude to the powers of sin and death from which we are freed only by the death of Christ in faith in God and his kingdom and hope for the overcoming of transitoriness in the resurrection of the dead. A theology of liberation must contain a criticism of all liberation understood in purely this-worldly terms. It must bring to light the ambivalences of the liberation slogans which have appeared in history, especially the fact that most dictators in world history have used the demand for liberation to mobilize the supporters without which they would never have been able to achieve their positions of power. This is bound up with the servitude of sin, because the liberators themselves are not free from the power of sin. That is why so often in history 'liberation' means merely the exchanging of one form of slavery for another – and only in fortunate instances is the latter not worse than the former. This is often associated with a caricature of social reality in the interest of the one who wants to emerge as a 'liberator' so that he can exercise power. One ideological weapon of this kind is the Marxist description of economic and social processes and conditions, especially Lenin's theory of dependence, according to which the prosperity of the industrial countries rests on the exploitation of the former colonies, nowadays the countries of the Third World. If theologians who often have only limited competence in economic questions because they have not sufficient specialist knowledge to form their own judgment uncritically take over the Marxist description of economic developments and conditions as a scientific account of social facts, then we have an uncritical assimilation to a type of secularism, moreover one which is also determined by enlightened atheism in all its economic assumptions and descriptions. Bound up with this is an understanding of liberation that puts in the foreground economic and political 'liberation' which on Marx's definition is by revolutionary action, and which plays down the biblical and theological aspects of liberation from sin and death, or even holds them out as the consequences to be expected from the political liberation which is to be realized first. Such a view confuses the Christian understanding of liberation with a this-worldly goal for liberation instead of making this latter the object of a critical discussion. Here we have an expression of the danger of false assimilation to the spirit of secularism which also applies to the themes of Christian 'orthopraxy': a commitment to change particular circumstances is first of all a concretization of Christian faith and of the hope for the kingdom of God which transcends this world. It then in fact easily comes to replace this hope, because people forget that the eschatological hope of Christians has its own specific quality which is the precise *opposite* of hopes which can be realized within the world; neither the resurrection of the dead nor the kingdom of God as the foundation of a society of true righteousness and final peace can be realized in this world through human action. To establish and develop that is the critical task of Christian eschatology in the face of secular and even revolutionary belief in progress, and in the face of ideological glosses and justification of the *status quo*.

Christian theology in the secular world must not give up central elements in God's transcendence of the world and in his salvation or allow them to fade into the background for the sake of assimilation to the secular understanding of reality. On the

56

other hand, Christianity may not be content with just securing the existence of the dogmatic content of the tradition. That would be merely to oppose a counter-world of faith to the secular world, not to bear witness to God as the creator and reconciler of this world of ours. It is a temptation for church and theology to regard as an opportunity for faith the readiness of human beings to succumb to the irrational, to an irrationally affirmed counter-world, as a result of a feeling of alienation in the secular world of culture. Flight from the meaninglessness of the secular world into irrationality can just as well turn to other religious and ideological elements and groups as to the church. The exotic attraction of such groups – like the Hare Krishna people, the New Age movement and also anthroposophy – is greater than that of the churches, which seem conventional alongside it. A church and theology which rely on a readiness to escape into the irrational on the part of those who are homeless in the secular world could very soon prove to be the loser. Rather, the opportunity for Christianity and its theology is to integrate the reduced understanding of reality on the part of the secular culture and its picture of human nature into a greater whole, to offer the reduced rationality of secular culture a greater breadth of reason, which would also include the horizon of the bond between humankind and God. In the theology of our century this task was perceived with great mastery by Karl Rahner, who thought that we should see that which is universally human in every dogmatic theme, but also perceive human need at the same time, and the way in which human beings are directed towards the divine mystery which has been manifested in Jesus Christ. A theology like that of Rahner is not of course concerned with just any form of rationalism. Indeed Rahner used to talk of the mystery of the divine reality which everyone is confronted with in his or her

57

personal life. But he did that in a rational way. From the beginning the link with reason has been part of the missionary dynamism of Christianity. In the Christian patristic period it characterized the claim of the gospel to universality against all the irrationalisms in which late antiquity was particularly rich. So I think that it is also important for the Christian controversy with the secular world to oppose the shortcomings of secular culture with a deeper and broader reason. By that means the apparent opposition between theonomy and autonomy will be done away with, and the great achievements of secular culture like the idea of tolerance and the rights of political freedom wil be preserved. This approach will also, however, have to overcome the clashes between confessions – had these not been so irreconcilable, modern secularism would never in fact have come into being. The continuation of divisions in Christianity gives the lie both to the spirit of the love of Christ and to the capacity of Christianity to achieve a breadth of reason which would be spiritually superior to the diminutions of secular culture. Therefore the ecumenical movement of our time, the movement towards a plurality of churches which mutually recognize one another within the community of the one church of Christ, is one of the basic conditions for a credible form of Christianity generally in the face of the secular world of culture which has emerged from the division of the church.

Bibliography

Karl Barth, *Protestant Theology in the Nineteenth Century*, Philadelphia and London 1972

P. and B.Berger, *The Homeless Mind, Modernization and Consciousness*, New York 1973

H.Blumenberg, *Die Legitimität der Neuzeit*, Frankfurt 1966

R.Bultmann, *History and Eschatology*, Edinburgh 1956

Harvey Cox, *The Secular City*, New York and London 1965

Wilhelm Dilthey, 'Das natürliche System der Geisteswissenschaften im 17.Jahrhundert', in *Gesammelte Schriften* II, Leipzig and Berlin 1914, 90-245

F.Gogarten, *Verhängnis und Hoffnung der Neuzeit. Die Säkularisierung als theologisches Problem*, Stuttgart 1953

Karl Löwith, *Meaning in History: The Theological Implications of the Philosophy of History*, Chicago 1949

– , *Weltgeschichte und Heilsgeschehen*, Stuttgart 1953

– , Review of H.Blumenberg (see above), in *Philosophische Rundschau* 15, 1958, 195-201

H.Lübbe, *Säkularisierung. Geschichte eines ideenpolitischen Begriffs*, Munich 1965

N.Luhmann, *Funktion der Religion*, Frankfurt 1977

W.Pannenberg, 'Christianity as the Legitimacy of the Modern Age. Thoughts on a Book by Hans Blumenberg' (1968), in *The Idea of God and Human Freedom*, Philadelphia 1973 (English title *Basic Questions in Theology* 3, London 1973), 178-191

T.K.Rabb, *The Struggle for Stability in Early Modern Europe*, New York 1975

T.Rendtorff, 'Säkularisierung als theologisches Problem', in *Neue*

Zeitschrift für Systematische Theologie und Religionsphilosophie 4, 1964, 318-39

–, *Gesellschaft ohne Religion? Theologische Aspekte einer sozialtheoretischen Kontroverse* [Luhmann/Habermas], Munich 1975

Max Weber, *The Protestant Ethic and the Spirit of Capitalism*, London 1977